SELF-CONFIDENCE AT WORK

Simple steps
to increase your confidence

Written by Julien Duvivier
Translated by Emma Lunt

Coaching 50MINUTES.com

HOW CAN I HAVE MORE SELF-CONFIDENCE?

- **Issue:** how can I assert myself and find fulfilment at work?
- **Uses:** having self-confidence allows us to express a natural authority that exudes from us, an assurance that will enable us to develop professionally.
- **Professional context:** career management, workplace relations, etc.
- **FAQs:**
  - During a meeting, how do I get the courage to speak to give my opinion?
  - My boss constantly belittles me. How can I be self-confident despite this?
  - How can I be more self-assured without seeming pretentious?
  - How can I ask my boss for a raise or promotion if I myself am not convinced of my own value?
  - How do I manage an experienced team when I have only just graduated?
  - How can I stay confident during a period of unemployment?
  - What attitude should I adopt when my colleagues refuse to work with me and make many petty remarks?

The increasing number of professional coaches and the new types of therapies highlight the fact that physical and psychological suffering In the workplace has become one of the main problems in Western societies. From the top manager

to the lowest employee, we all have difficulty thriving professionally and we experience a series of frustrations that
often translate into a lack of self-confidence.

This issue of self-confidence within our professional activity
firstly involves reversing an assumption that is still widely
accepted today and affirming, in the words of the psychologist and psychoanalyst Roland Guinchard, that "work is a
personal experience that is experienced collectively and not
the other way around"[1] (Guinchard, 2011: 1).

Here we find the increasingly widespread idea that our work
has to be the expression of a private and profound desire (a
subconscious force that drives us to work) so that it is no
longer seen as a "job", an inescapable constraint to which
we are subjected. In order to get away from this logic of
"we're all in the same boat", which makes work miserable
and unfulfilling, it is a good idea to explore what motivates
us and what defines us personally to ask ourselves this
question: how can my work make use of my self-confidence
and become a place of accomplishment?

This short guide aims to get you to ask yourself the right
questions and to enable you to freely explore the paths that
will lead you to climb the professional ladder in accordance
with your most profound aspirations. You will also find
practical tools enabling you to quickly affirm yourself in
your daily work.

---

1. This quotation has been translated by 50Minutes.com.

UNFAILING CONFIDENCE: THE BASICS

SELF-CONFIDENCE; A COMPLEX IDEA

Different meanings

Self-confidence as a concept first appeared in the writing of William James (1842-1910), an American psychologist considered to be the father of psychology in the United States, in his work *Principles of Psychology*, which was published in 1890.

According to him, self-confidence is the opinion that we have of ourselves regarding what we have done. This perfectly summarises the state of mind that today dominates the Western world and that tends to represent the individual as a disembodied object: we would thus be subjected to the same laws as an organisation or a state whose results are measured by turnover or gross domestic product (GDP). This is an entirely external self-confidence, based on appearance, and its limitations can be seen in the simple fact that even the performance indicators of organisations and states tend to increasingly involve our wellbeing as employees and citizens in their assessments.

Starting from this behaviouristic perspective as developed by William James, which defines the individual as the product of what they do, being self-confident is the result of a collection of behaviours and results that can be observed from the outside. Although it is absolutely true that our professional achievements, demonstrated through concrete and visible results, are closely linked to our feeling of self-confidence, is this definition not an overly-restrictive view that tends to categorise us? Are winners not always losers someday, and vice versa?

Self-confidence has another meaning which, without excluding the analysis of external behaviours as a determining sign, prefers to approach the issue around the idea of self-belief. Through this concept, we can connect self-confidence with a collection of characteristics that the first approach did not: believing in ourselves gives us the opportunity to have confidence in our desires, our hopes, our strengths and our reference points to act. We advance securely, with the firm assurance that there is a strength within us which exists without necessarily needing to prove itself. And it is this energy that enables us to have a positive influence on the outside world and to take the risk to affirm ourselves.

The constellation of self-confidence

In his work *Croire en soi ou la confiance perdue et retrouvée* (*[Believe in yourself or confidence lost and found]*, 2004), the psychoanalyst and psychosociologist Jean-Claude Liaudet introduces the idea of the "constellation of self-confidence" by asking the following questions: "What difference is there between self-confidence, self-esteem and self-love? How does knowing oneself contribute to self-confidence and assurance, to self-affirmation?"[2] (Liaudet, 2004: 35).

Indeed, we tend to confuse self-confidence, self-esteem and self-love with being sure of ourselves, asserting ourselves, accepting ourselves and knowing ourselves. We have the impression that all these terms are the same, and it is for this reason that we often struggle to understand why we are incapable of reacting in the way we want to when faced with a professional situation that makes us lose self-confidence. We can try to understand the challenges of each element of this constellation by viewing it as a process.

---

2. This quotation has been translated by 50Minutes.com.

The constellation of self-confidence

Self-awareness
"Know yourself": this precondition is essential if you want to build your self-confidence on solid foundations. This lifelong journey enables us to become aware of our potential and limits.

Self-acceptance
A similar idea to self-confidence, self-acceptance is about accepting yourself as you are, seeing what displeases you about yourself without rejecting it or resorting to self-accusation.
This awareness also enables you to see your qualities with humility.

Self-love
This idea goes beyond any moral judgement: I am **capable of loving myself as I am**. Aware of your imperfections, you can use them to improve yourself every day and take advantage of those around you.

Self-confidence
This a feeling of **security**. Like a child that shows blind confidence in their parents, the individual knows that they can trust themselves.

Self-esteem
In esteem, we find the idea of **value**, a value that can be financial, moral, spiritual, etc., depending on the Individual.

Self-affirmation (assertiveness)
In any professional sector, assertiveness is the must-have skill for any person looking to be recognised as an expert in their domain. There is no need to manipulate, be aggressive or run away in case of difficulties: you have enough self-confidence to **impose your leadership with kindness and authority**, respecting your limits and those of others.

Although they are defined differently, it goes without saying that these ideas intermingle and interact with each other. As a consequence, none of what is said above should be taken as a rigid process with fixed steps: depending on the history and specificities of each individual, a particular path must be followed to gain self-confidence.

SELF-ANALYSIS: THE GORDON TEST

Thomas Gordon (1918-2002) was an American psychologist and a pioneer in conflict resolution. Drawing heavily on Abraham Maslow's (1908-1970) work on the satisfaction of needs, he conceptualised the idea of "win-win". According to him, seeking to understand the other person will have a direct impact on self-assurance.

The Gordon test can be useful for any person wanting to know themselves better with the aim of gaining self-confidence in their professional life. It enables them to analyse their own self-confidence in order to have a starting point for self-reflection.

Thus, you are asked to respond as spontaneously as possible to a series of suggestions (such as "life is just power relationships and fights", "I can listen and do not cut people of", "When I disagree, I dare to say it calmly and to make myself heard", etc.) with "fairly true" or "fairly false", while thinking in terms of working life. According to these results, a general trend will emerge from your reactions in the face of situations that put your self-confidence to the test. You will be able to see if you are more evasive, aggressive, manipulative or assertive.

GOOD TO KNOW

Assertiveness or assertive behaviour is an idea that was introduced in the United States in the domains of psychology and psychiatry, and which broadened into personal development during the 20th century. To assert means to affirm yourself and defend your rights, therefore avoiding any behaviours of fleeing, submitting or manipulating.

This test never aims to reveal an accepted truth about yourself. On the contrary, it enables you to reflect on what you judge to be the current state of your behaviour at work in order to give you points for improvement and to begin a process that will take you much further.

FINDING HELP

While being aware of a lack of self-confidence and seeing how this weakness manifests itself is already a significant step, detecting the origins and making this introspective step towards wellbeing productive is a whole other, much more laborious, matter.

At this stage, all sorts of fundamental questions can appear: am I really made for this job? How can I develop in my position despite the mountain of difficulties that lie ahead of me? How can I make a professional shift without endangering my career? It is difficult to answer these without external help.

Professional organisations

Some organisations offer individual or collective guidance meetings to enable everybody who wants to focus on their professional situation to see it more clearly. Through regular interviews over a period of time defined by your counsellor, you can share your questions about a specific problem or your general situation. These courses are free and aim to enable you to get to know yourself better thanks to conversations with the guide and personal work on analysing your professional aspirations. Your meetings must be sufficiently spaced out to allow daily life and changes to fuel your reflection on questions such as: what are my failures and successes? What are my motivations? What are my values? Which hypotheses on professional development relate to me? etc.

Coaching

Coaches appeared during the 1990s and for a while they remained a privilege for top managers wanting to improve their image. Since the 2000s, the practice of coaching has become popularised (as shown by the many professional certifications delivered by a plethora of training institutions: SF Coach, ICF, EMCC, etc.) and many middle managers have used this type of guidance to boost their career.

Unlike psychoanalysis or therapy, guidance from a coach is brief (a few months of guidance at the most), while still enabling the person to obtain measurable results almost immediately. While the use of coaching can be useful for people who encounter problems that do not profoundly challenge them, it does not seem appropriate for a person who has identified a real lack of self-confidence. In fact, even when supplemented by certified techniques such as neurolinguistic programming (NLP), coaching rarely allows an individual to find the resources necessary to free themselves from what stops them from expressing themselves. In this case, the work will be much longer and will undoubtedly call for the intervention of a specialist.

Therapy

You know that anybody who questions why they cannot assert themselves at work needs to carry out a genuine analysis, a deep search into the origins of the 'non-belief' in themselves. Learning to know yourself, to accept yourself and to love yourself is not a step that you take with the sole aim of developing professionally.

When we are not self-confident at work, we often make the mistake of focusing on someone who belittles us or something else that overwhelms us. We do not see past the problem that is in front of us and we seek to overcome a situation that we have often subconsciously provoked ourselves. As such, a logic of escape takes us away from the real questions: what am I doing to make these people feel authorised to encroach on my 'territory'? Where does this flaw in my self-confidence come from?

To stop accusing others and ourselves, to escape repetitive logic that sends us around in circles and stop us from developing, it is necessary to pull the weeds out by their roots, in a way, by returning to the source of our lack of self-confidence. It is often found in childhood; therapy is therefore necessary to get into contact with the bad thing that is eating away at us and stopping us from reaching our full potential.

Choosing psychotherapy, psychoanalysis or behavioural therapy depends on the preference of the individual. The only rule is that you must choose your therapist well: beyond the importance of the method used (which must suit you), this person must inspire confidence in you and you must want to work with them (for some months up to many years!).

AFFIRMING YOUR DESIRE

The restoration of self-confidence means that each individual must confront the obstacles that keep them from their desire at work: they must go in search of their vocation to be able to express all their potential and their profound aspirations at work, including (and above all) the most hidden ones. This desire to work is often buried under a pile of negative words that has been building up since birth. The phrase "You will be a good doctor, son" can be as destructive for a young boy who aspires to be a baker as the traditional "you are a good-for-nothing".

GO FOR YOU

"Lech-Lecha" (Genesis 12:1): this Hebrew expression means "Go for you". The divine order to the first patriarch Abram is clear. He is called upon to leave everything (country, family, homeland) to go to the country that the Lord, his God, promises him. Often transcribed as "Go from your country", the expression can in reality be translated literally as "go for you". It is only by answering this call, by expressing a desire that is bigger than ourselves, that neither our family nor our homeland (nor our colleagues) can define for us, that we can become more self-confident.

Learn to say no

In her bestseller *L'intelligence du cœur* ([*Emotional Intelligence*], 1997), Isabelle Fillozat speaks about the positive anger that everybody is better off expressing to move towards their true desire and learn to assert themselves. Expressing this 'healthy anger' enables us to resolve a systematic evasion of conflict (running away, denial) or a violent response (which seeks to respond to attacks with accusations). It therefore consists of self-affirmation without rejecting or judging others, and expressing yourself using the pronoun "I" rather than the accusation "You".

The author gives the example of a woman who is victimised by a superior who is abusive and misogynistic in exercising his authority. According to her, expressing this positive anger would involve saying: "When you call me 'little one', I feel uncomfortable because I need to feel your respect, you are my manager and I would prefer for you to call me by my name, I would feel happier working with you."

Thus, before learning to say "yes", it is vital to go through the stage that the founder of analytical psychology, Carl Gustav Jung (1875-1961), calls 'individuation'. This allows us to leave any relationship in which others seek to take over us and which does not enable us to get out of our comfort zone.

THE ORIGINAL JOY OF LIFE

"If a baby has just been born, it is because they are confident about life"[3] (Liaudet, 1998: 1): how can we not see this statement from the most famous children's specialist as a sign that each of us have shown (at least once) a joy for life, an elementary confidence in what happens? Leaving our mother's womb is primarily an act of faith – the first manifestation of self-confidence and of a refusal to die. Before congratulating the parents, do we not welcome the newborn with all the kindness and recognition that it deserves? It has just confidently experienced what specialists recognise as being the first trauma, the first confrontation with reality. This reminds us of the challenges and obstacles that are littered along the path to restoring self-confi-

---

3. This quotation has been translated by 50Minutes.com

dence at work.

This step can seem frightening and not very rewarding in the short term: we risk a lot and are not sure of getting what we want. In reality, it is not an option. By once again using Fillozat's example, imagine that this employee wants to be trusted with more responsibility. Do you think that she can avoid putting her manager in his place? Does she not, by seeking to develop without taking this first step of resisting embarrassment, risk entering a vicious circle that will lead her to increasingly depend on this man? What she gains in professional development on paper will translate to reality through an even greater submission to this abusive authority.

Individuation is a central idea of Jungian thought. It can be defined as the process of the natural formation of the psychological individual, which is a separate being from the collective psychology. The first step of individuation is differentiation; we understand from this term that, according to Jung, we cannot become a free individual without taking the risk of saying the 'no's that enable us to position ourselves in front of another person or a group as a separate, differentiated person.

Restoring your desire

Anybody who claims to know themselves perfectly is totally wrong. Everybody who has done real and serious introspective work will tell you that this idea is a fantasy: we have to deconstruct what we believe to be our desires and our personality in order to move towards a more authentic relationship with ourselves and our work. To do this, we must dare to question our certainties, our way of thinking and our relations; in short, everything to do with our accepted truth which stops us from understanding what is really happening in a given situation.

With this in mind, every difficulty faced at work can be valuable material for analysis. Three time periods should be separated.

1. **Observation time:** in what situation, facing which individual and in what way does my lack of self-confidence show at work? As part of this, it is strongly recommended to keep a logbook of your observations. Writing notes on the situations that seem confusing to us enables us to restore order where chaos reigns. Ideally, you should make a habit from the start of proceeding in three time periods: setting the scene (a), identifying emotions (b) and noting the words that come to mind (c). For example:

   "I had lunch with Mr B. today. It was torture! I don't know why this man makes me feel uncomfortable (a). I was hot, I didn't know what to do with my hands, I constantly felt the threat of being laid bare (b). It was as if a voice was constantly saying to me: 'You should realise that you are not capable

> of managing his fortune. How can a man of his calibre trust
> somebody like you?' (c)"

2. **Analysis time:** am I right in thinking that this situation or individual is an opportunity for me to fail? Where does this fear come from? This is where we bring our feelings face to face with the reality of the situation. To do this, we have to focus on what is happening in our internal world. At what point does this very real situation make me lose self-confidence? What past situations am I currently reliving through what is happening right now? What is the voice inside my head telling me? To continue with our asset manager's logbook, this is what this kind of analysis could look like:

> "What did this man do to make me feel uncomfortable? I don't understand. Beyond the fact that he was much more well-dressed than me, he did not seem to want to belittle me. He even seemed kind. A bit too kind actually... It's strange, I have the feeling that he was trying to show me that he was my equal. This reminds me of the evening meals I used to have with my family: when it was my turn to talk about my day, my father continually cut me off and outdid all my stories. I often told myself that I could never compete against him. I felt useless."

3. **Action time** on reality: think, speak and work differently. Once we have passed from fantasy opinions to reality, a major part of the work is already done: although we are still uncomfortable due to a lack of self-confidence, we have demystified the situation and have the tools at our

disposal to resolve it. This internal voice that drives us to be only a mockery of our true selves is unmasked. A process has already begun that will enable us to face the situation differently. The following could be the result of such work a few weeks later:

> "Mr B. came to the office today. It's funny, because I visited my parents last Sunday and I noticed that my father was still trying to outdo me, as if he felt threatened. I spoke to him about it and although we did not reach an agreement, speaking about it made me feel great! This morning, I was another man with Mr B.: he effectively tries to intimidate me by dramatising his life, which is his way of being confident... But now, this no longer bothers me at all, and I would even say that I enjoyed myself. Finally, he signed the contract and wants to recommend me to an associate."

Expressing your desire

Daring to go for what we really want and daring to head towards risk by expressing your desire demands an effort that can seem unnatural: it is a bit like declaring your love to somebody who does not know about your feelings. We risk being rejected, scorned, mocked, etc. But without this risk, we stay in the fantasy that we know what the other person is thinking better than they do and hold onto the illusion that we share a bond with them.

Facing reality is always beneficial. Daring to tell this person what they deserve to hear means demonstrating self-confidence and showing the other person that we respect them: by shutting ourselves away in a fantasy ("He/she is going to fire me if I tell them about my need to develop", "My team leader does not have the courage to ask human resources for my promotion", "I must work badly since that he/she never trusts me with big projects", etc.), we also make other people prisoners.

ACCEPTING DISTURBANCES

"Impose your chance, hold tight to your happiness and go toward your risk. Looking your way, they'll follow." (Char, 1983): sometimes, without being aware, those close to us are the first to make us doubt our journey. In the workplace, this person may be a colleague who is not very used to seeing us thriving and dynamic, a manager who feels that they are losing control, etc. Each person will make you aware, in their own way, consciously or subconsciously, that you are scaring them and that they do not like it. You must do it: authentic self-confidence is also about accepting disturbances. We end up taking a certain pleasure from it.

Although getting closer to the other person to share our desire with them (climbing the ladder, changing our way of working, communicating differently, etc.) is a difficult step, speaking is always freeing and creates meaning.

Expressing an authentic desire at work often scares us and many factors can make us refuse to impose our chance. While it is certain that the process of restoring self-confidence does not happen in a day, another much more gratifying certainty exists within you and you have the opportunity to go and find it.

The desire to work is a quest, a search for meaning that will enable you to know yourself better and to accept yourself as you are so as to acquire self-confidence built on solid foundations.

TOP TIPS

- **Take time for yourself outside work** by doing a cultural activity or a sport, for example. This will enable you to take a step back from your daily life. Often, by throwing ourselves into a new activity, our self-confidence is surprisingly boosted.
- **Rid yourself of negative language,** such as "I am fat", "I am stupid", "I've always been lazy", etc. Put what you think to the test by writing down everything that comes to mind on a piece of paper. Insofar as all of this does not come from you, but from an opinion that has been imposed on you, there is nothing left for you to do but to rip them up and destroy them as much as you want before finally throwing them in the bin. You are free!
- **Breathe!** Regularly think about focusing on your breathing. Inhale deeply and exhale slowly, visualising the movement of air that travels through your body. This is an exercise that enables you to restore your internal security.
- **Be a healthy mind in a healthy body.** Think as much as possible about eating well, and avoid too many caffeinated drinks (coffee, fizzy drinks). Learn to consider your body as a sacred temple which you must take care of.
- **Make to do lists.** Give yourself attainable and realistic objectives every day. Once a task has been achieved, cross it out and feel the satisfaction of having completed an objective.
- **Create a success box.** We tend to quickly forget our successes. Make a habit of putting pieces of paper stating

your daily victories in a box.

- **Repeat after me: "I am fearfully and wonderfully made".** Take time to look at yourself in the mirror every morning and say this phrase as if you were saying it to somebody you love. In this statement taken from the Book of Psalms (Psalms 139:14), we find the essence of self-love: every one of us, both unique and imperfect, carries something marvellous. You will end up believing it... and for good reason!
- **Do not get involved in gossip and power games.** These can be entertaining, but it is a very bad way to let off steam that will get you caught up in a vicious cycle and will distance you from the first source of satisfaction that you should take from your work: reaching your objectives.
- **Take real breaks.** No matter your workload, take at least ten minutes per half-day to totally disconnect (including from your phone) and use this freedom: go for a walk, chat with a colleague over a tea/coffee, read, etc.
- **Take holidays.** Holidays are a right for every worker and a must for every person that wants to shine and show themselves as responsible in their work.

FAQS

DURING A MEETING, HOW DO I GET THE COURAGE TO SPEAK TO GIVE MY OPINION?

Firstly, be aware that not all opinions are always good to give. Show good judgement by asking yourself if the frustration of not having the courage to speak comes from genuine shyness or if it is more linked to a desire to exist and be recognised, even though you have nothing relevant to bring to the topics being discussed.

In the first case, dive straight in: speaking in public must be learnt, and there are techniques and introductory phrases that you can prepare in advance. Plenty of charismatic personalities were unhealthily shy, or may even have had a stutter, during their childhood! In the second case, you must do more in-depth work to find the root of this existential emptiness that drives you to want to be seen at any cost. While you are working out what is happening here, abstain from speaking: you risk talking but saying nothing.

MY BOSS CONSTANTLY BELITTLES ME. HOW CAN I BE SELF-CONFIDENT DESPITE THIS?

If your superior belittles you, they are undoubtedly the one who lacks self-confidence, for their own reasons. The best thing to do is to have a meeting with them so as to assertively explain how this situation is holding you back. It may be that your conversations are constructive and the two of you make up. It is also likely that this interview results in a conflict, but you will have at least expressed your desire and gained assertiveness. If the situation gets worse, get help from a staff representative or speak to human resources.

HOW CAN I BE MORE SELF-ASSURED WITHOUT SEEMING PRETENTIOUS?

Be careful not to give yourself too much self-confidence: this generally conveys "overcompensation" linked to... a lack of a self-confidence. Being unaware of your weaknesses by making others responsible for your difficulties or giving yourself all the credit for teamwork, for example, are signs that will not only be taken as personal attacks by your colleagues, but that will also make you lose all credibility.

HOW CAN I ASK MY BOSS FOR A RAISE OR PROMOTION IF I MYSELF AM NOT CONVINCED OF MY OWN VALUE?

Here we see the main advantage of the success box (see 'Top Tips'): regularly taking the time to take an inventory of your successes. Whether they are quantifiable or not, these achievements are arguments that you can bring to your management to justify your request. Take into account the fact that any manager or team leader worthy of this name is happy to their teams: not showing you the appreciation that you deserve will be a source of frustration for them. Give your employer a chance!

HOW DO I MANAGE AN EXPERIENCED TEAM WHEN I HAVE ONLY JUST GRADUATED?

If you were hired it is because you were judged capable of facing the challenges of the position. Demonstrate interpersonal intelligence: an individual who rebels against your authority is certainly doing it because they think that you have nothing to teach them. And this is true from a technical point of view: they know their department much better than you. Show them that you appreciate this know-how while staying firm in the system you have implemented. Managing a team means above all creating synergy between knowledge and know-how to achieve objectives.

HOW CAN I STAY CONFIDENT DURING A PERIOD OF UNEMPLOYMENT?

The thing that we usually miss during periods of unemployment is structure and a social life. Structure your day. Organise your schedule and do not let the emptiness engulf you: alternate between research time and relaxation time, set yourself attainable objectives, see friends, etc. Furthermore, make the most of the situation to clear your mind and do the things you dreamed of doing when you were working. And do this without guilt!

WHAT ATTITUDE SHOULD I ADOPT WHEN MY COLLEAGUES REFUSE TO WORK WITH ME AND MAKE MANY PETTY REMARKS?

Relations in the workplace can be very complicated and sometimes remind us of the playground. This is precisely what is happening: your colleagues are replaying a scene from their past... and you probably are too! If no conversation is possible, do not play into their game and take the necessary step back by helping yourself or going to find help from a specialist. If the situation becomes unbearable, speak to any qualified person in the company or to occupational health services: some situations can go very far if you do not quickly get a hold of them.

OVER TO YOU

THE INTERVIEW

Ask five (kind) people to answer the questions below. You will have a sample of the way you are perceived by the outside world. Use these answers as a working tool.

- If you had to briefly introduce me, how would you describe my personality? My way of working?
- What do you think are my main qualities?
- Give an example of a situation when one of these qualities was particularly evident.
- If you had to give me advice for the rest of my career, what would you want to tell me in terms of my areas for improvement? What about in terms of my professional development?

EXPAND YOUR NETWORK

- Are you interested in a certain position at a certain company? Do you know somebody who could tell you about it in more detail? If so, have the courage to invite them to lunch, do not miss out on the opportunity to find out more, and do not feel guilty for "using" this person: they will probably be delighted to put you into contact, to give you information, etc.
- Do not neglect online professional networks such as LinkedIn: take the time to see what positions exist in your sector and create virtual links with people who could one day play a specific role in the advancement of your career.

- Do not look down on interns and young professionals: firstly, because, being on the path to confidence, there is no reason for you to be contemptuous of anybody else, but also because anybody may one day want to return the favour.

MAKE THE MOST OF YOUR TALENTS

- Does everybody tell you that you should sing? Sign up for a choir or take classes.
- Do people say you have green fingers? Make a vegetable patch or a botanical wall.
- Have you always wanted to learn to play the piano? There is a reason for this desire: you must try it.

These untapped talents are frustrations that you undoubtedly reproduce at work: you must free your creative potential to free your connection with work.

We want to hear from you!
Leave a comment on your online library
and share your favourite books on social media!

FURTHER READING

BIBLIOGRAPHY

- Bellanger, L. (2009) *Développez votre confidence en vous.* Nogent-le-Rotrou: ESF éditeur.
- Char, R. (1983) *Œuvres completes.* Trans. Bard, E. Paris: Gallimard.
- English Standard Version of the Christian Bible (2007) Illinois: Crossway Books.
- Fillozat, I. (1997) *L'intelligence du cœur.* Paris: JC Lattès.
- Guinchard, R. with Arnaud, G. (2011) *Psychanalyse du lien au travail. Le désir de travail.* Paris: Elsevier Masson.
- Lacroix, M-J. (2013) *Vivre et travailler avec des personnalités difficiles.* Paris: InterÉditions.;
- Le Temps des Managers. (2010) *Test de Gordon.* [Online]. [Accessed 25 January 2016]. Available from: <https://letempsdesmanagers.files.wordpress.com/2010/03/test-de-gordon-etes-vous-assertif-_.pdf>
- Liaudet, J-C. (1998) *Dolto expliquée aux parents.* Paris: L'Archipel.
- Liaudet, J-C. (2004) *Croire en soi ou la confiance perdue et retrouvée.* Paris: L'Archipel.
- Pasini, W. (2002) *Être sûr de soi.* Paris: Odile Jacob.

ADDITIONAL SOURCES

- James, W. (2000) *The Principles of Psychology: Volume 1.* London: Dover Publications Inc.
- Jung, C. G. (1955) *Modern Man in Search of a Soul.* Trans. Dell, W. S. and Baynes, C. F. New York: Harcourt Harvest.

- McGee, P. (2011) *Self-confidence: The Remarkable Truth of Why a Small Change Can Make a Big Difference.* London: Capstone.
- *Psychologies* website: https://www.psychologies.co.uk/work>

DOCUMENTARIES

- *Le bonheur au travail.* (2015) [Documentary]. Martin Meissonier. Dir. France: Productions Campagne Première. eng